W9-CBV-240

The Soulful Money Manual

The Soulful Money Manual

9 KEYS TO BEING EFFECTIVE, HAPPY AND AT PEACE WITH MONEY

DR. RICHARD MITZ

Health Communications, Inc.
Deerfield Beach, Florida

www.hci-online.com

Library of Congress Cataloging-in-Publication Data

Mitz, Richard

The soulful money manual : 9 keys to being effective, happy, and at peace with money / Richard Mitz

   p.   cm.

ISBN 1-55874-908-X (tradepaper)

1. Finance, Personal. 2. Finance, Personal—Religious aspects—Christianity. I. Title.

HG179.M553 2001

332.024—dc21

©2001 Richard Mitz

ISBN 1-55874-908-X

Publisher: Health Communications, Inc.
           3201 S.W. 15th Street
           Deerfield Beach, FL 33442-8190

Cover design by Lisa Camp
Inside book design by Dawn Grove

CONTENTS

ACKNOWLEDGMENTS

Many good souls have made this book possible. First, a special thanks to Ron and Mary Hulnick, who have been an inspiration. They have assisted me in gaining the true meaning of financial freedom. I appreciate both their generosity and their giving me so many of the keys presented in this book. John-Roger and John Morton, my spiritual teachers, have shared their wisdom and guidance with me and I am deeply grateful to them. I thank my children, Stacy, Danny and Jeffrey, who bring me so much joy. I love them so much. They are my shining lights. And the most heartfelt thanks to my wife Phyllis, my beloved, who is always showing me the way to more loving and upliftment.

PREFACE

WHY ANOTHER
BOOK ON MONEY?

Don't we have enough of these self-help, get-rich-quick books? There are plenty of them on bookstore shelves. However, do they have a spiritual focus? Do they emphasize that in relationship to your finances, God is your partner?

This book does. It contains a very unique set of techniques and methods that I call keys, which have been proven to help solve money challenges. Whether you have lots of money or you're in debt, using the keys presented in this book can help bring you to that special place inside you that knows how to work well with money.

HOW DO YOU FEEL ABOUT MONEY?

Do you wish you had more money? Do you long for those days when you were debt-free? Do you find yourself searching to be content with your financial situation? Like everyone else, I, too, had issues with money.

I grew up in an upper middle-class family. My parents had concerns about money. We lived well but worried we would never have enough money, no matter how much we had. As a teenager and college student, I felt an internal pressure, a worry: How am I going to make a living? Would I ever have enough?

I chose my profession as an oral surgeon, in part, because I knew it would provide me with a secure financial living. There were times, during my training, when I was in debt and would invest in very risky ventures so I could "make my fortune" and not have to worry again. I never did make that fortune. In fact, I went into greater debt. Even after I was a practicing oral surgeon making a nice salary, I still took foolish risks and kept losing money. I knew I had to do something differently.

What finally shifted my old pattern with money was gaining the wisdom to practice the combination of keys presented in this book. I found a formula that worked.

As soon as I performed all nine keys together, a whole new world unfolded for me. I was no longer worried about money. In fact, I had so much excitement and joy that a deeper level of freedom with money came forward. I was happy and at peace with money and my net worth skyrocketed.

SO HOW DO YOU KNOW THAT THESE NINE KEYS REALLY WORK?

I had to know if these keys would work for others, so I did some research. I recruited a variety of people ranging from those who were in major debt, to people with substantial incomes. Every single person who actually used the keys found a big change in their lives regarding money within a ninety-day period.

Angela's story: credit-card-debt-free

Angela was maxing out her credit cards. While she lived a nice life outwardly, inwardly Angela always had a nagging feeling about her debt hanging over her. She could usually distract herself from those concerns, but when she was honest with herself, she could feel that pull, that uneasy feeling. That pull, although subtle, really did not allow her to be at peace or be happy—not just with money, but also in other parts of her life. She agreed to participate in my research

project, and worked with the techniques. After practicing
the program for ninety days, she evaluated her
progress. In all three categories (peace, happiness and
effectiveness), she improved.

Angela found that she was clearly more effective
with money. Not only had she stopped going deeper
into debt, which had been her long-term pattern; she
was actually beginning to pay down her existing debt.
When asked if she was happier with money she
reported, "Yes. I am enjoying it more. I'm happy to
save, happy to spend—it is more special now." She
addressed the question: "After doing this program, do
you find you are at peace with money?" by answering,
"Yes, I have a gentle, almost fun place inside of me,
more trust that money is available perfectly for me."

Penny's story: reaching financial freedom

Penny started the program in debt and described
her financial situation as "feeling very depressed and
angry. . . . I decided that I could no longer afford to

be on the financial merry-go-round." After using the keys for ninety days she wrote, "I feel freedom from stress. I have a sense of direction and I know where I want to go and what I want to do in my life as far as my finances go."

Jake's story: no more worries

Jake was another test participant who was doing well outwardly, making a very handsome salary. However, he related that inwardly his attitude toward money was "marked by a sense of struggle and a major source of worry." He had a daughter who was going to a private school and was preparing for college. Jake had put some money away, but had concerns about the future—in particular, having adequate college tuition for his daughter. After completing ninety days' work with the keys, he reported feeling "more effective with creating the opportunities that generate revenue." When asked about his degree of happiness, Jake wrote, "Yes, I am treating money more as a game

now, rather than totally as a worry or a problem."
When asked to evaluate his level of peace after being
on the program he responded, "This has been one of
the major areas where I am experiencing change. I
have a greater sense of peace . . . a greater trust."

My Wish

These are just a few of the examples of people who
actually performed the keys. I found, no matter where
participants started in relation to money or no matter
what their financial issues were, when they followed
the keys, they were more effective, happy and at peace
with money.

My wish is that this book helps others gain the
freedom and joy that I have in my life since I began
practicing the nine keys.

AUTHOR'S NOTE

The *Soulful Money Manual* presents nine keys to creating a relationship with money that produces peace, happiness and effectiveness. I share the keys with you in the form of a parable. In the parable, I use words and concepts that mean different things to different people, depending upon their spiritual or religious upbringing. I use words like God, Soul, consciousness and so on. I encourage you to move beyond personal or traditional interpretations of these words or concepts and focus on the actual techniques presented.

Have fun and go for the freedom.

INTRODUCTION

It was April 5, 1951, in Earth time. I was about to be born on the planet Earth and was getting ready for what lay ahead. It looked like I was going to be an oral surgeon in this lifetime and had chosen Jewish parents, two sisters and a brother. I was going to be in a male body. My life pattern was taking shape. I had a feeling this was going to be a special life, but I wasn't sure why.

Suddenly, there was a knock at my door. Who could that be? I had all this preparation to do before I went to Earth. As I opened the door, I was shocked to see one of God's special angels. What could she want? Did I miss something? Why would God send one of his special agents to me?

You have to understand. This was not a run-of-the-mill angel. This being of light was very rare, not just in beauty, but in duty. When this type of angel was present, you listened and listened well.

I asked, "How may I help you?"

The beautiful angel smiled and gave me a note. She said, "God rarely sends messages like this—it must be very important."

My knees began to shake. My breath and pulse quickened. I tried to be present and attentive. With as much might as I could muster, I thanked the messenger and closed the door.

What was going on? My head swirled. I sat at the edge of my bed and began reading the note.

Dear Richard,

I have a special assignment for you on Earth.

I am sorry this is such short notice. I know this is a busy time for you. I hope you can see me tomorrow at 10:00 A.M.

Love, God

This was beyond belief. I had heard about this happening to other souls, but I never thought it would happen to me. This was such an unusual experience, yet, after reading the note, I felt total peace. I just sat back and stared at the sky in wonderment.

I was looking forward to my meeting with God.

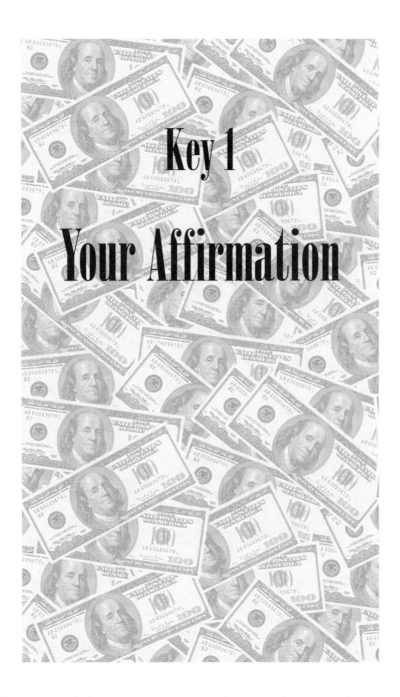

Key 1

Your Affirmation

When the time came on the next day, I was taken down a large hallway, through many, many clouds. The angel and I walked through the biggest doors I had ever seen. The doors opened toward us. As I walked through these doors, I saw the most amazing sight I had ever seen. There was God. He was magnificent beyond words. Such beauty. The love I felt for him was beyond compare. He invited me in. He was so gracious. He asked me to sit next to him so he could talk with me. Needless to say, I was overwhelmed.

"Son," he said, "I have a special mission for you on the planet Earth."

I was surprised he wanted me to do something special.

"Father," I replied, awestruck, "I will do anything for you."

I was wondering if when I left his presence I would feel the same way. I know sometimes I agree to things that later surprise me.

"On Earth, there is so much pain and misunderstanding around something that should be enjoyed and cared for," he began.

I thought, *There are so many things on Earth that are like that.* I wondered what he was referring to.

"What might that be?"

"Money," he replied.

I thought, *Are you kidding? Of all the things on Earth, why would he focus on money?*

"Money, throughout the history of Earth, has been so abused, it has become a negative focus instead of a positive one," he explained. "Your job is to create a manual that brings it back into the beautiful, supportive tool it was designed to be. I will spend time with you, before you are born, explaining the simple keys that will make money so easy to have. These keys will bring a peace and ease to all who follow them. They will bring about a healing around money and what it represents."

I took a deep breath and swallowed hard.

"Are you sure you have the right guy?" I asked him with some uncertainty.

"My son, would I make a mistake?"

"Of course not, Father, it was just that I don't know if I'm qualified to do such a task. You know how hard it is to change things there. Souls generally find when they are born, they forget about you and what they're there to do," I replied.

He assured me, "Don't worry. It will all be taken care of."

"I sure hope so!"

"Why don't we get started, Richard?"

Who was I to say no?

"Money is so very precious. It has to be nurtured and cared for. It has to be respected and treated responsibly. I want everyone to have as much as they need. If my children follow these keys, I will make sure they are effective, happy and at peace with money," he said.

My interest was piqued. I was excited to get going.

God began to spell it out. "Key number one is very simple. I, God, am everyone's partner. I want to assist everyone on the planet to have infinite abundance. Your biggest challenge is helping people know and believe that. So, I will give you several ways to tell people how to come to the awareness that they know I am their partner."

"What are those ways?" I asked.

"First, they have to create an affirmation."

"What exactly is an affirmation?" I asked.

"Affirmations are brief, constructive, positive statements that, through repetition, help to change beliefs. You don't even have to believe them when you start repeating them. I'll give you an example. 'God is my partner, taking care of me and taking care of everything I need' or 'God is my source, and I am open to receiving large sums of money with ease and grace.'"

"How does it work?"

"You will be repeating your affirmation one hundred times each day for thirty-two days. The repetition helps your consciousness build faith and positive attitudes toward me, God, being your partner."

"I think I understand," I responded. "Could you explain more about how an affirmation teaches me that you are my partner?"

"This technique, practiced daily, helps change limiting beliefs around money by reinforcing the positive attitude stated in the affirmation. Remember, one hundred is the magic number. One hundred times per day repeating the affirmation, for thirty-two days in a row. You can say them all at once or spread them out through your day, but it must be at least a hundred times.

"Once people get the idea, they can make up their own affirmation along these lines. You see, Richard, individuals have to begin to change their consciousness. All they need is a small change in direction. This will get it moving. The words must be chosen carefully. They have to be very positive and clear," he concluded.

Seeing that he was pausing, I quickly jotted down this key as something important to do once on Earth. I assumed this key would be part of the manual I was preparing at God's request.

THE TO-DO LIST

1. a. Create an affirmation with
      God as your partner.

   b. Say the affirmation one
      hundred times a day for
      thirty-two days.

   c. Create other affirmations
      about money and abundance
      if you wish.

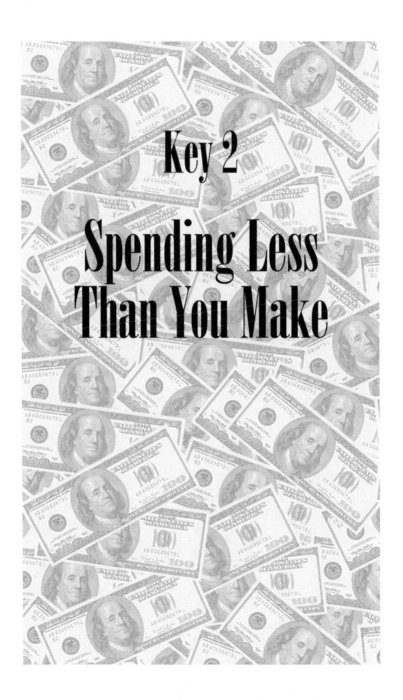

Key 2

Spending Less Than You Make

I was enjoying my time with God. The process of beginning to work with God as my partner was so fulfilling. I knew that when I got to Earth, I would have to do my affirmations to connect back to the knowledge that I am not alone and God is really my partner, taking care of me and taking care of everything.

After a while, he started to explain the second key.

"Richard, on Earth, money has a life of its own. It has to be treated a certain way to make it work for you, instead of you working for it. In order for money to respond to you in a positive way, you have to be responsible with it," he began.

"How do you do that?" I asked.

"You have to be accountable for how you spend your money."

I was puzzled. "What exactly does that mean?"

"It means that you have to spend less money than you make," God explained. "This shows your consciousness that you are taking responsibility. Once this is accomplished, your relationship with money is established in your consciousness differently. Money can begin to work for you."

"What would be the first step in making sure you spend less than you make?" I wanted to know.

"To become aware of what you spend your money on," he said. "Watch every penny that you spend. You see, my son, as soon as you see where your money has been spent, you begin to evaluate what is necessary and what is frivolous. That is not to say you should *judge* what is frivolous, but you should begin to prioritize what is important to you," God explained patiently. "As soon as you become accountable with your money, there is an opportunity for less waste. It is almost automatic that you will save at least 5 percent of your money when you become aware of what you spend it on."

"Father, I want to be clear on this. Would another way to say this be to create and stay on a budget?"

"That would be the next step in this key, Richard. First, bring your awareness to where your money goes and then decide, on a monthly basis, where you want to spend your money. Remember, as soon as you do this with the intention of having more money coming in than going out, you will see a magical transformation."

"This seems easy up here," I exclaimed, "but on Earth—well, things can be quite challenging down there."

"That is very true," he agreed. "Once you start to budget and stay with it, while practicing the keys, an amazing freedom comes over you with regard to money. You see you are taking care of it, being responsible. Money will then be very different inside of you. Money will want to work for you." He studied me closely. "I can see by your expression, Richard, you don't believe me."

"Father, please don't misunderstand," I said. "I want to believe you. It's just that it seems that everything on Earth is set up for you not to want to be responsible and track your money and create a budget."

"You are right, in a way. However, if you do achieve this goal of tracking your money and following a budget, there is so much reward that comes with it. Have you ever accomplished a challenging goal?" he asked.

"Sure."

"How did you feel?"

"I felt wonderful," I remembered. "I had accomplished something and felt fulfilled and complete."

"You got it. That is what will happen as you perform this important key. You will receive many gifts on many levels. You will feel like you have control over your money, instead of money controlling you."

"Thank you. It's an honor doing this assignment with you."

"Richard, this will help many people. When people follow the nine keys, they will have mastered a very challenging aspect of living on Earth—their finances. The next key is a very easy, fun key."

I wrote the second key down.

THE TO-DO LIST

1. Keep saying your affirmation one hundred times per day for thirty-two days.

2. a. Start tracking what you spend your money on, and create a budget so you can start spending less than you make.

   b. Have the clear intention of staying within your budget.

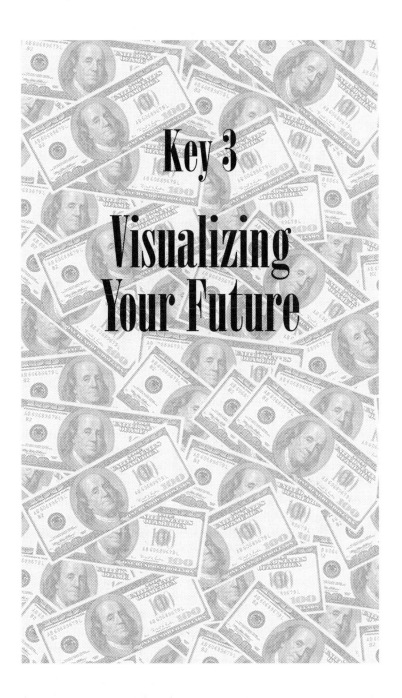

Key 3

Visualizing Your Future

G od started right in.

"This next key, my son, will be an easy key to follow. It is very important to work with this key every day."

I was excited to hear this next key. So far, I thought the keys that God had given me seemed pretty practical.

"There are two steps to this key, and two conditions I ask you to place on it. First I'll explain the steps," he said. "The first step is to visualize exactly what you want in your life, but from a unique perspective. You have to imagine that the life you want has already transpired six months out into the future."

Wanting to be sure I understood, I asked, "Can you give me an example?"

"Well, imagine you are an adult. You would take an important event that will take place six months from the present, perhaps your birthday or a big event that you will be attending. At that event in the future, you are talking to someone who is important to you about what has taken place during the last six months of your life. Be as creative and lifelike as possible in your visualization. Make this so real in your imagination that it is as if it has already happened in your life.

"The details that you explain to the person you are talking to are what you would really like to actually have taken place in your life. In other words, in your imagination, you are pretending six months of your life have already happened. Act as if six months out is the present. Let's actually do this exercise together," he invited.

"Okay, I will give it my best," I said.

"It's six months from now, and I am standing in the   lobby of a hotel where I'm attending a big conference," I said, voicing my visualization. "I am talking to my wife, telling her how great our lives have been these last six months. Our health is great, and we have so much abundance. We have increased our wealth by 20 percent in the last six months. I have followed all nine keys of abundance God entrusted me with. They were so easy to implement, and they have been very effective. It has been magical how my attitude about money has changed. I feel prosperous. I have much more money coming in than going out. I have so much overflow that we can give to others. There is money coming in to me from many unexpected sources. I really know God is my partner. It is amazing."

"Richard, you've got the idea!" God seemed pleased. "You can make your visualization as detailed as you want, and you can add other things besides money issues. You can add things about relationships, health, happiness, etc."

"You see," he went on, "your visualizations give *me* a road map to follow so we can be co-creators. I need the map of where you want to go so I can help you get there. You use this visualization every day until you actually reach the date of the event you had set for that visualization. Then you create a new one detailing what you want to take place six months out in the future from that point."

"Father, you said there were two steps to this?" I asked. I was paying close attention.

"The second step is to do an additional visualization for three to five years out as well. It doesn't necessarily have to be as specific. It can take less time than the six-month visualization and be less detailed if you wish," he explained.

"This will help you establish more direction on where you want to go in the future. Let's do another example."

"Okay," I agreed.

"I see myself three years down the road on vacation with my family," this visualization began. "We are staying in a beautiful hotel because I have so much money I can afford it with ease. I feel wonderful about my life and am at peace with money and my relationships. I am telling my wife how enjoyable these last three years have been together. We have much greater health, and we are happier than ever before. The children are also doing well. We've been able to give abundantly to others in many ways, and that has led to blessings for many people.

"We have accumulated so much wealth over the last three years. It has been amazing how powerful and effective the keys have been. The keys were instantly easy to follow three years ago when I started the program.

"During the last three years, I have come to know deeply that God takes care of me and is my partner," I concluded.

"Very good," God noted. "These visualizations can take less than a minute each day. Now, there are two important qualifications to doing your visualizations. The first is you have to declare, after the visualization, 'this, or something better Lord, for the highest good of all concerned.'"

"So, by saying 'for the highest good of all concerned,' that's another way of saying to you 'bring it to me if it's for my best—if it's not for my best, I don't want it. Right'?" I asked.

"Yes," he replied. "The other qualification is that the visualization should be at least 50 percent believable. A way to test this qualification is to imagine something so 'out there', it is really only 1 percent believable. Then, refocus back to around 50 percent believability and see how much more at ease you are with the road map you have created for me to follow."

I thought about the visualization process he described and asked, "Are there other ways to do this exercise for those who find visualization challenging?"

"Yes, Richard. For example, you can write a story that describes the vision of your imagined life for both the six-month and three- to five-year time frame. Use the same qualifications I mentioned, and read it each day. For some of my children this will be more effective than the visualization exercise," he concluded.

"Thank you," I said.

I was enjoying this experience. God. Money. What fun. How wonderful. I felt so free. I was getting words of wisdom on how to work on the planet. I added the third key to the list.

THE TO-DO LIST

1. Keep saying your affirmation one hundred times per day for thirty-two days.

2. Track your money and follow your budget.

3. Start doing your six-month and three- to five-year visualizations every day. Begin very simply at first if you wish. An example would be seeing yourself very happy and content with your financial situation.

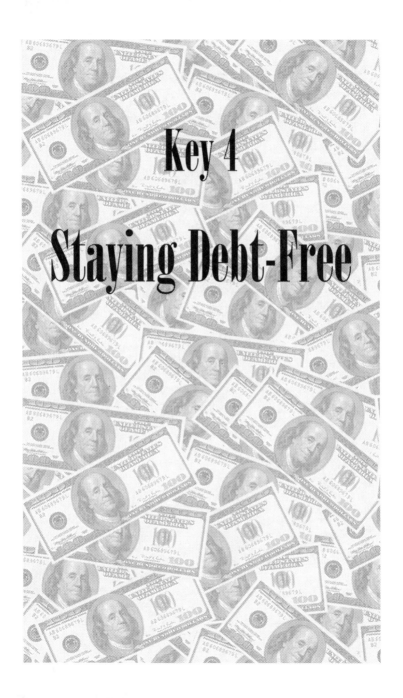

Key 4

Staying Debt-Free

G od began again.

"This next key, my son, can be the most challenging key."

"What key is that?" I asked.

"You have to be financially debt-free. The way Earth is set up, debt is a negative game. It basically robs you of your future gains. You are mortgaging your future, spending money from your future monetary gains. That can make it difficult to be effective, happy and at peace with money.

"This negative game of debt can keep you in bondage to money rather than having money work for you.

"Being in debt can be very addictive. You see, you

can be seduced by glamour, possession and short-term desires, and you can lose sight of how easy and joyful creating wealth can be." God explained.

I could see by his expression how concerned he was. He indicated over and over again that getting out of debt is so important to financial freedom. He also emphasized that you should not judge yourself, however, for being in debt. At the time of finding yourself in debt, you—like others in debt—are doing the best you can, God assured me.

"If you are already in debt, what do you do?" I asked.

"You have to stop," he said in no uncertain terms. "In the short term, you do not necessarily have to pay back debt to see a dramatic change in your financial environment. You just have to stop going into debt.

"Once you stop accumulating debt, you have made a major shift in your consciousness. You are putting a stop to the negative game. You are no longer participating.

"This is so important. This will change your whole

dynamic of money on the planet Earth. Things will start changing rapidly, and initially you might experience some challenges. There could be a variety of tests that come forward. Just take one step at a time and pray for my assistance. Do this as often as you wish. I will be there to help you—and remember, help can come in many ways. Be patient and observe what goes on. Once you get through it, you will see a whole new level of freedom come forward," he said, with total assurance.

"Father, after a person stops going deeper into debt, isn't it important to get out of the debt they've been carrying?" I wanted to know.

"Yes. However that can be accomplished with the use of all the other keys. In other words, practicing the budgeting, visualizations, etc. The real key here is to stop going deeper into debt and have the desire to pay the debt back. It will happen over time."

God paused again, so I quickly jotted this key down.

THE TO-DO LIST:

1. Keep saying your affirmation one hundred times per day for thirty-two days.

2. Track your money and follow your budget.

3. Do your six-month and three-year visualizations every day.

4. Stop going into debt—get help with this if necessary—and create a plan to pay back your debt.

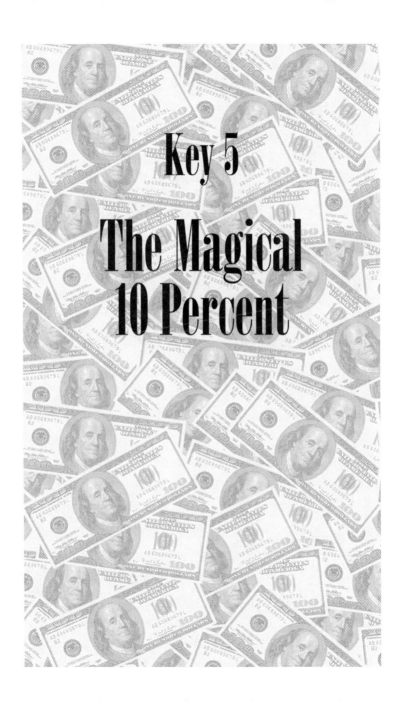

Key 5

The Magical
10 Percent

Before we went on to the next key, God spent a lot of time emphasizing how being debt-free could be considered by some as the most important key. Just following this one key could change many lives.

The love and light coming from God was beautiful.

We then went on to the next key. It was divided into two specific steps.

"Richard, on Earth there is a magic number that will help you to create wealth and have happiness and peace with money," he said with an intriguing look.

"What number is that?" I really wanted to know more.

"The number ten," he said simply.

"How do I apply that on Earth?" I asked.

"Every time you make money, you must immediately, without delay, pay yourself 10 percent of what you made," he said. "This money is set aside from the rest of your finances and is called a money magnet or wealth account."

I was puzzled. "That doesn't make any sense, Father. If I'm making money from working, isn't that my money already?"

"In a way, yes. I'm talking about something different. You use your money to buy things and provide yourself and your loved ones with the necessities of life. These obviously are important," he said.

"However," God continued, "sometimes the line between necessity and desires gets very blurry. Desires generally are related to an emotional response, and they can masquerade as a need. Needs are what you have to have in order to survive on Earth. I want you to understand there is nothing wrong with short-term desires. As long as you can maintain your 10 percent money magnet/wealth building account, you can handle your short-term desires any way you want."

With uncertainty, I asked, "Can you give me an example?"

"Let's say you walk into a store on Earth, and you see a special coat. You fall in love with it. You think and feel you have to have it, but do you really need it? Not really; it is a desire. You can certainly get along fine without this particular coat in terms of taking care of yourself and keeping warm (real necessities). But the coat represents a short-term desire you are experiencing. The coat has piqued your emotions, so you want to buy it. If it is within your budget, you can relax and say to yourself, 'I have enough for this.' If it is not in your budget, you can relax and realize that you are creating long-lasting qualities of peace and happiness as you stay within your budget while walking away from the coat." After he explained this example he continued.

"First, you purchase your necessities and then your short-term desires (that fall within your budget) from the 90 percent portion of your income," he said.

"The remaining 10 percent of your income, that you are now paying to yourself, is to be used for long-term goals, such as saving for retirement, investing in a house, paying for your children's college education and so on. This 10 percent is not spent on short-term desires.

"The 10 percent you put away will serve you well. It will act as a magnet to draw more money to you and your wealth account. It will seem like a miracle has unfolded after you are in the habit of doing it.

"For it to really become easy for you to do, I recommend you include the 10 percent you pay yourself in your budget. Automatically write out a 10 percent check from your paycheck. And remember to add this to your visualization.

"The 10 percent monies you give to yourself can become very precious. When paying yourself 10 percent becomes more important than your short-term desires, you have 'made it.' It becomes a priority, and nothing will stand in the way.

"The action of maintaining a money magnet/

wealth account creates a special feeling within your consciousness. It can contribute greatly to your happiness, peacefulness and, of course, your effectiveness with money. That 10 percent will also begin to grow on its own and act as a magnet for more and more money. There is an ancient proverb on Earth: 'Money begets money.' When you have money, additional opportunities to make more money come about. Money has a life of its own, and it will begin to multiply very rapidly once that magical 10 percent is put away."

I felt such a sense of gratitude for what God was doing for all of us. This was very magical.

THE TO-DO LIST

1. Keep saying your affirmations one hundred times per day for thirty-two days.

2. Track your money and follow your budget.

3. Do your six-month and three-year visualizations every day.

4. Stop incurring debt and work with your plan to become debt-free.

5. Pay yourself 10 percent of everything you earn into your money magnet/wealth account.

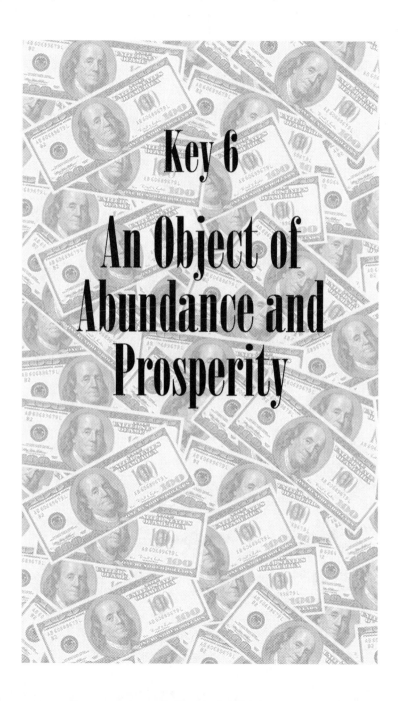

Key 6

An Object of Abundance and Prosperity

As I was organizing all the keys in my mind and writing them down on the to-do list, a question came to me.

"Father, this seems so easy. Why is it that when you get to Earth it becomes so challenging?"

"Believe it or not, this can be easy. Let me show you how it works," he offered.

"On Earth, people are programmed to work to make money. It is universal that you have to work for a living. People might not like it, but it is accepted and it is done.

"Now, let's reframe the idea that working on this program on Earth and dealing with money is challenging.

"This financial program takes several minutes a day

to practice most of the keys. Initially some keys, such as the affirmations and budgeting your money, take perhaps several hours per month. If you are willing to invest a short amount of time in yourself, you can make a profound impact in your financial matters. In fact, the time you spend on the keys could have a greater effect than working all week. So if, in your mind, you can frame these procedures as being more effective than working a job, why not take the time to perform these keys at least several minutes a day?

"You will only be taking perhaps an average of ten minutes a week to change your whole world. Most jobs are about forty hours per week and are done without question. This practice, which I am sharing with you to pass on to others on Earth, takes about ten to twenty minutes per week and could have a greater effect on personal happiness and peace than those forty hours spent at work!

"Practice these keys for several minutes daily with the understanding that this is a blessing from me, God. I want you to have more joy and happiness than you have ever imagined! These keys can contribute to that. Isn't it worth ten to twenty minutes each week practicing the keys, when you are willing to work all week for your job? Make it easy on yourself. Take the easy way out. Practice the keys," he concluded.

"Wow, I never looked at it that way—forty hours for work. I can end up making more money working the keys for ten minutes a week. It is really amazing," I said as I began to understand the power of the keys more deeply.

The more time I thought about this insight, the more I realized how important this information would be. I had to make sure I remembered all of it.

"What is the next key?" I asked, hungry for more.

"It is a very easy key."

God explained, "You have to find an object that symbolizes abundance and prosperity. It can be one object or several objects—just so it is some thing or some place you can see or be in regularly. This is so whenever you see it, you are unconsciously and continually reminded of prosperity and riches. It will remind you of abundance and bring you a sense of gratitude for what you have. Gratitude is a magical energy. When you are grateful for something I will bring more of it to you. That is the way it is set up. Keep focusing on what you have and be grateful and more will come to you."

"Can you give me an example of an object that symbolizes abundance and prosperity?"

"It will vary for each individual, and it can depend on where each person is in his or her financial progression. One good example, is one of my children has a special glass object on her desk. The object didn't cost a lot of money, but it was very beautiful and well made. When she looks at it, she has such a good feeling. It reminds her of God being her partner, and she experiences infinite abundance," he said.

"Another person's object is more of a practice—keeping fresh flowers in her home. It is in her budget and gives her such a sense of well-being. It reminds her consciousness of how much she really does have and how grateful she is for this abundance.

"Another 'object' could be a house if it is within the budget. Owning the house could symbolize for the homeowner his ability to take charge of his money so that every time he walks into the house, he's reminded on some level of the abundance and gratitude in his life. An office might provide the same experience for someone, awakening that gratitude for the particular space, the work it represents, the accomplishment, or other aspects of prosperity.

"The list goes on and on. It can be as simple as a gold coin or even an accumulation of cash. What is important is that you go inside to find what symbolizes prosperity to you. Ask your consciousness to bring it forward, when the timing is right, and ask that it be clear and within your budget. The answer can come quickly or within days. Just be patient and trust it," he concluded.

I was already thinking about what on Earth would be my object to remind me of abundance. I was getting excited about going back to Earth. *After all, God is my partner,* I thought, while adding another key to the list.

THE TO-DO LIST

1. Keep saying your affirmations one hundred times per day for thirty-two days.

2. Track your money and follow your budget.

3. Do your six-month and three-year visualizations once each day.

4. Stop incurring debt and work with your plan to become debt-free.

5. Pay yourself 10 percent of everything you earn.

6. Find an object that expresses and awakens your sense of gratitude for your abundance, prosperity and riches. Bring that object into your everyday life. Make it a fun process.

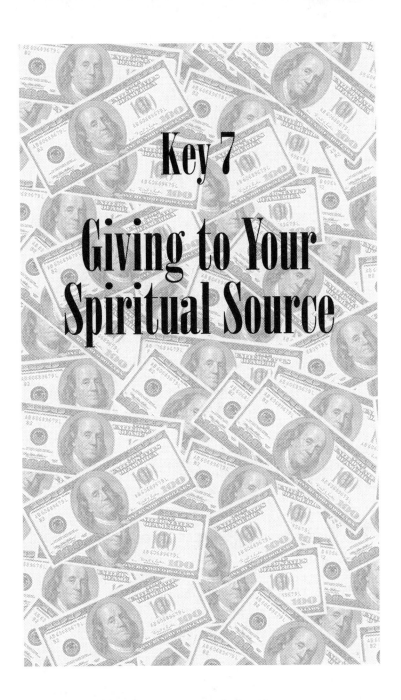

Key 7

Giving to Your Spiritual Source

"The next key, Richard, is knowing who is first in your life," God began.

"What do you mean?"

"We have to let each individual know that there is more than enough, and that I will supply infinite abundance to you. It is vital that this be demonstrated as clearly as possible on Earth. With the demonstration to all parts of the consciousness, magic will happen." He once again caught my imagination.

"Father, who is first in our life when we are on Earth?"

"Why, I am," he said simply. "If you can demonstrate the trust and faith that I am first in all areas of your life, and that I am your source, I will then give back to you a hundredfold. I will keep giving you more and more blessings."

"How can I demonstrate my trust and faith in you?" I asked.

"Remember the magic number of 10 percent?"

"Yes, but that was giving 10 percent of your income to yourself."

"That is true, and that practice is very important. An additional key, that is just as important, is giving 10 percent to me. This has been called tithing in some religions," he intoned.

"How can I do that?"

"If you give that 10 percent to your spiritual source or where you receive the Word of God, whatever you consider that to be, that is good enough for me."

"You mean like your church or temple?" I asked, vaguely remembering something about ancient Hebrew history.

"Yes. The source that gives you my Word—your spiritual inspiration—whatever that is for you. That is all you have to do, and you will see magic unfold."

"What kind of magic?" I asked, intrigued.

"Magic appears many different ways. I'll give you several examples: For one person, magic might express itself as a sense of ease around money. Another one of my children finds that this practice is one of the most important things in his life. He finds it's an insurance policy—he knows if he gives his 10 percent to his spiritual source, then I will clearly take care of him and his family—and because of his faith and trust, I do.

Tithing might bring forward the experience of greater inner knowing, awakened intuition or a strong sense of grace. Other outcomes might be greater health, a clear sense of purpose, more loving or a greater connection to the soul." And still another would be the magic coming back financially a hundredfold.

"Father, with all these 10 percent payments to myself and to you, I will never have enough to pay my bills!" I protested, getting a little worried for the first time.

"If you do all the keys and are patient with the

process, you will have more than enough money and resources. You see, you have to use your creative ability, the visualizations and so on, to create more money coming in than going out. Include in both your six-month and three-year visualizations into the future that you have more than enough money coming to you to pay at least 10 percent to yourself and 10 percent to God. It will happen. Initially you can stage it."

"What do you mean?" I asked, as my worries were quickly eclipsed by my curiosity.

"As long as you start the process of giving a percentage to yourself and to me with the intention of getting to 10 percent, things will start to change. You can proceed in stages to effect a change in your behavior, start moving in a new direction, and then your consciousness will begin to shift into prosperity and abundance."

Inwardly, I was beginning to have some concerns about the ease of implementing this program on Earth.

"It sure seems challenging to me, even from here." I voiced some doubts.

"Son, have faith and allow a new approach in your life to unfold."

The worries were dissolving again in his presence. I jotted down this latest key and noticed the to-do list for Earth was getting clearer and clearer.

THE TO-DO LIST

1. Keep saying your affirmations one hundred times per day for thirty-two days.

2. Track your money and follow your budget.

3. Do your six-month and three-year visualizations every day.

4. Stop incurring debt and work with your plan to become debt-free.

5. Pay yourself 10 percent of everything you earn.

6. Find an object that expresses and awakens your sense of gratitude for your abundance, prosperity and riches. Bring that object into your everyday life.

7. Tithe 10 percent of your income to your spiritual source, or the source of God in your life.

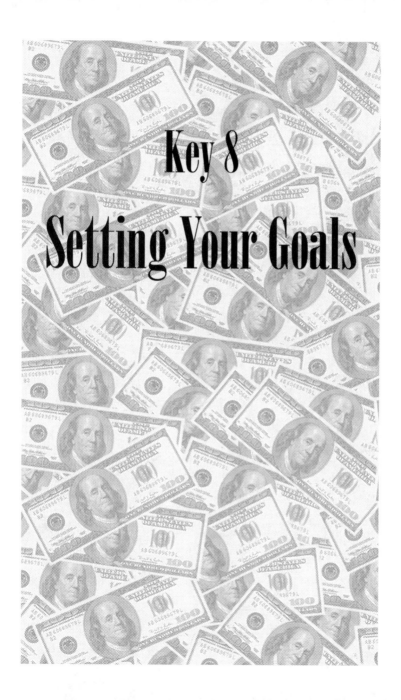

Key 8

Setting Your Goals

"The next key will have to be practiced at least once a week," God said. "You will want to place on paper the exact financial goals you want to achieve over the next year."

"Do you mean decide what you want your salary and income to be for the next year?" I asked.

"Exactly. You also want to write out how much you want to accumulate in your money magnet/wealth account, how much you want to receive in gifts, etc. It has to be at least 50 percent believable. Feel free to be expansive and to experiment. Let me show you an example," he said as he handed me a sheet of paper.

INCOMING MONIES FOR NEXT YEAR	
Next year's salary	$ 40,000.00
Wealth account increase	$ 6,500.00
Special gifts from unexpected sources	$ 2,500.00
Total Income for Year	**$ 49,000**

TOTAL ACCUMULATED VALUE OF MONEY MAGNET/WEALTH ACCOUNT FOR NEXT YEAR

$38,500

He explained how to use this.

"You want to focus on the financial goals list at least once a week. You could leave it on your desk, and look at it when you start work in the morning.

You can add as many categories as you wish. Perhaps there are special projects you can add (including the elimination of debt).

"Father, what does this mean?" I asked, pointing to

'Special gifts from unexpected sources' on the list.

"That's a good question, Richard. Be open to receiving from unexpected sources. Some examples would be an unexpected tax break, an inheritance, a bonus, or a forgotten debt paid back. Or, it might be a gift of great value. Don't limit yourself. Allow yourself to be surprised."

"What a good idea," I said.

This key will anchor your financial goals and allow them to manifest on the planet," he added.

THE TO-DO LIST

1. Keep saying your affirmations one hundred times per day for thirty-two days.

2. Track your money and follow your budget.

3. Do your six-month and three-year visualizations every day.

4. Stop incurring debt and work with your plan to become debt-free.

5. Pay yourself 10 percent of everything you earn.

6. Find an object that expresses and awakens your sense of gratitude for your abundance, prosperity and riches. Bring that object into your everyday life.

7. Tithe 10 percent of your income to your spiritual source.

8. Create a table or list of your specific financial goals for the next year. Focus on them at least once a week.

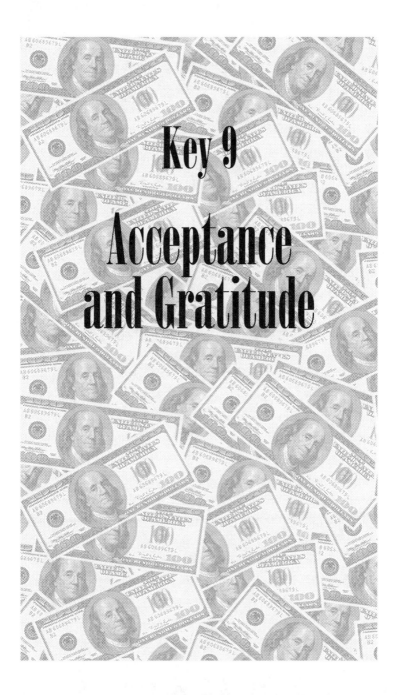

Key 9

Acceptance
and Gratitude

I was beginning to realize that my meeting with God was almost over. I did not want it to end. I enjoyed being with him and receiving his incredible wisdom and guidance. I knew this meeting would always be with me, and I was very excited at the thought of sharing it with others.

"This last key is very important. You see, this key applies to life in general," God shared.

"What is that key?"

"The key is accepting your financial situation. Acceptance does not mean that you don't want things to improve. Remember, your money and financial situation is not good or bad—it just is. Bless your situation and know that you can take control of money by following all nine keys.

"Gratitude is one way to assist you in coming into acceptance. Gratitude is a magical energy on Earth."

"What do you mean?" I asked.

"When you are feeling lack and focusing on what you don't have, you create blocks in your consciousness. When you have blocks, I cannot give you what you want as easily. When you begin to focus on what is working in your life or what you already have, your consciousness begins to expand and opens up to receive from me. I can bring so many more gifts to you."

"You mean if I move into gratitude about the things present in my life, like the love and the material abundance I already have, instead of what I don't have, I will begin to feel better inside? And then you can bring me more of what I want out of life?" I asked.

"Yes, and you can be as specific as you wish. I will give you an example. Let's say you are feeling and thinking that you don't have enough money to do something special. You are focusing on lack. Start focusing on being grateful for special things you already have: You have shelter, friends, loving relationships . . . you have your health. You always can find something to be grateful for. You can be as specific as you wish. In fact, you can make a list."

I found this idea very interesting.

"The next part of gaining acceptance is to make sure you do not judge yourself or anyone else for your financial situation. You have to move into forgiveness of whatever judgments you have inside of yourself. This will free you to move forward with loving." God paused while I absorbed this.

"What happens when you judge?" I asked.

"Judgments against yourself or other people cause a constriction or contraction in your consciousness. In order to release those constrictions and bring more expansion and freedom to your consciousness, you can use forgiveness.

"It can be a very effective tool as you go through

life. When you forgive your judgments of yourself or others, that part in your consciousness that you've locked up with judgments opens, allowing more joy, happiness and peace inside of you."

"Wow," I replied, "but I don't really understand how that would work. Could you give me another example?"

"Certainly," God said, and I was touched by his infinite patience. "Say you are judging yourself as being irresponsible for having gotten too far in debt. While you will certainly need to demonstrate your responsibility by working to eliminate the debt (as I explained in Key 4), you can also gain more freedom in your thoughts, feelings and attitudes by forgiving yourself for any judgments you have around your indebtedness.

"Anything you judge about you or someone else can be released through this action of forgiveness. Just say sincerely to yourself, 'I forgive myself for judging myself as being irresponsible with money.' As you begin this process, you may notice other judgments that need forgiveness. You might need to keep repeating forgiveness statements for a while. Once you release the judgments that pull or constrict your consciousness, you will experience a greater ease and freedom. It might take some practice."

"Can forgiveness and gratitude be used to gain acceptance in all parts of a person's life, not just in their finances?"

"Exactly. These are very powerful tools that can assist you throughout your life on earth."

I felt blessed that God was giving me these tools to enjoy life so much more.

I added this to the list as well.

THE TO-DO LIST

1. Keep saying your affirmations one hundred times per day for thirty-two days.

2. Track your money and follow your budget.

3. Do your six-month and three-year visualizations every day.

4. Stop incurring debt and work with your plan to become debt-free.

5. Pay yourself 10 percent of everything you earn.

6. Find an object that expresses and awakens your sense of gratitude for your abundance, prosperity and riches. Bring that object into your everyday life.

7. Tithe 10 percent of your income to your spiritual source.

8. Create a table or list of your specific financial goals and focus on them at least once a week.

9. Come into acceptance and gratitude about your present financial situation. Forgive any judgments around money. Repeat, as often as it is needed.

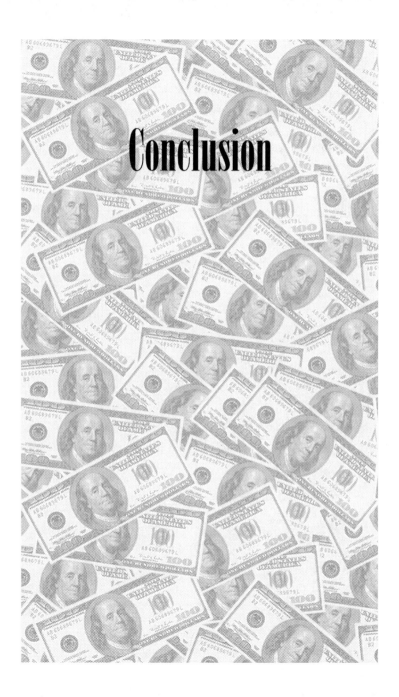

Conclusion

My visit with God was coming to an end.

"These, my son, are all the keys you will need to bring you and others happiness, peace and effectiveness with money. If my children follow these keys their lives will become easier and more graceful. Perhaps initially it can seem like a lot of work. Once they start practicing the keys and seeing the results, it will become easier and easier," God assured me.

"Father, I only hope I can do an adequate job in presenting the keys. It would be an honor to make this material known."

"The opportunity will present itself. Do not worry." Once again, he reminded me, "I am your partner."

"I love you, Father."

"I love you, too. I love all my children. I want them to have abundance, prosperity and riches. It is their divine right."

This was such a special moment. I was within hours of coming to Earth, and I was so excited about my new mission: Assist others to become free with their finances and to facilitate them in having effectiveness, happiness and peace with money. What a life!

THE TO-DO LIST:

1. a. Create an affirmation with God as your partner.

   b. Say the affirmation one hundred times per day for thirty-two days.

   c. Create other affirmations about money and abundance if you wish.

2. a. Start tracking what you spend your money on, and create a budget so you can start spending less than you make.

   b. Have the clear intention of staying within your budget.

3. Start doing your six-month and three- to five-year visualizations every day. Start very simply at first if you wish. An example would be seeing yourself very happy and content with your financial situation.

4. Stop going into debt—get help with this if necessary—and create a plan to pay back your debt.

5. Pay yourself 10 percent of everything you earn into your money magnet/wealth account.

6. Find an object that expresses and awakens your sense of gratitude for your abundance, prosperity and riches. Bring that object into your everyday life. Make it a fun process.

7. Tithe 10 percent of your income to your spiritual source, or the source of God in your life.

8. Create a table or list of your specific financial goals for the next year. Focus on them at least once a week.

9. Come into acceptance and gratitude about your present financial situation. Forgive any judgments around money. Repeat as often as it is needed.

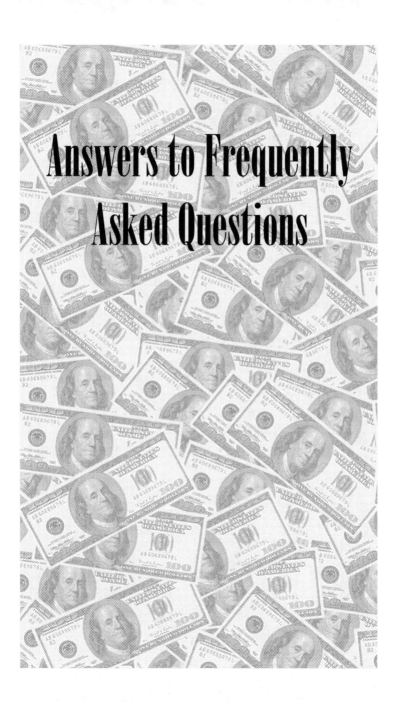

Answers to Frequently Asked Questions

1) **Is it necessary to do all the keys at once?**

Answer: Generally I have found that doing all the keys at once seems to make a greater difference than doing them one at a time. When all the keys are done simultaneously, something very magical happens.

It can be a challenge to start and to continue practicing all of the keys at once. Here's a suggestion: Do a portion of all of the keys at once. Write out all nine keys and set up how much of each key you are going to practice the first week with the intention of doing all the keys in perhaps ten weeks. An example is:

1. Start saying a simple affirmation such as "God is my Partner." Within several weeks, you can add more detail to the affirmation if you wish.

2. Go over your checkbook and make categories for each type of expense you have, to form a table for an eventual budget. Within weeks, you will have an actual budget.

3. In your six-month visualization, see yourself talking to a person who is important to you about how much fun you had in doing *The Soulful Money Manual* program and how successful you now feel. Within several weeks, you can elaborate on the scene.

4. And so on.

You want to take at least microscopic steps on each key.

If you cannot do all the keys at once, go within and listen to your inner knowing and decide what is the most crucial step for you to start with.

2) Should you use your money magnet/wealth account to pay down your debt?

Answer: The most financially sound answer is to take your 10 percent and pay off your debt. However, I feel the best way to handle that is to use a portion of the 10 percent wealth account to pay back your debt and to deposit the other portion into your wealth account. This way you are training your consciousness to do both things: get rid of debt and also build wealth. When people do both, this adds to their sense of accomplishment.

This is something that you can experiment with and see how you do.

3) How long does it take for this program to begin to work?

Answer: I have seen it take as little as a few weeks to several months. If you practice the nine keys with diligence and discipline, eventually the program will "kick in." All you need is to change direction; even microscopic change over time will result in great change in your consciousness. For some, patience might be what's learned from doing these keys.

4) Are these nine keys the only steps I have to follow?

Answer: I would recommend these as the minimum. There are so many great ideas and exercises out in the world with regard to finances. I am sure they can be effective. Through experimentation, I found that these keys work very well together. They seem to complement and enhance each other.

5) Is it important I believe in the keys before I use them?

Answer: Not at all. Just follow them as if it were a recipe for a cake. Just do them consistently and, if possible, with joy. Make them fun.

6) How long should I do the program?

Answer: I would suggest for the rest of your life. Eventually, it will become a habit. In my experience and, from my research, I found if one step is skipped your financial situation might not change dramatically, but it can affect the final outcome. If you miss some of the steps, little things begin to change and as time goes on, the changes get more noticeable. These changes can affect—perhaps undermine—your effectiveness, happiness, and peace with money. I would encourage keeping up with it all the time. It becomes very routine and easy. It becomes a part of life.

7) Is having a mortgage on a house considered debt?

Answer: Technically, yes. However, it is collateralized as an appreciating asset, so it does not qualify as debt in this program. In fact, energetically and psychologically, it could be used to enhance the program for some people, as buying a house can represent prosperity and financial stability to their consciousness, assuming it is within their budget

8) **Once I've experienced positive results, what should I do if I fall back into my old behavior and habits with money?**

Answer: As soon as you become aware that you're off track, review the nine keys. First, use Key 9— don't judge yourself. Practice forgiveness as needed, moving into gratitude for what you've already accomplished. Then, go back to Key 1, and do your affirmation. Finally, start making microscopic changes that re-establish the practice of the other seven keys.

Enjoy your way to greater effectiveness, happiness and peace with money. Have fun!

Celebrate Family

#1 New York Times
BESTSELLING AUTHORS
Jack Canfield
Mark Victor Hansen
Marci Shimoff
Carol Kline

Chicken Soup for the **Mother's Soul 2**

More Stories to Open the
Hearts and Rekindle the
Spirits of Mothers

Code #8903 • $12.95

Winner! "Favorite Book"
#1 New York Times
BESTSELLING AUTHORS
Jack Canfield
Mark Victor Hansen
Patty Hansen
Irene Dunlap

Chicken Soup for the **Kid's Soul**

101 Stories of Courage,
Hope and Laughter

Code #6099 • $12.95

#1 New York Times
BESTSELLING AUTHORS
Jack Canfield
Mark Victor Hansen
Jeff Aubery
Mark Donnelly
Chrissy Donnelly

Chicken Soup for the **Father's Soul**

101 Stories to Open
the Hearts and Rekindle
the Spirits of Fathers

Code #8946 • $12.95

#1 New York Times
BESTSELLING AUTHORS
Jack Canfield
Mark Victor Hansen
Patty Hansen
Irene Dunlap

Chicken Soup for the **Preteen Soul**

101 Stories of Changes,
Choices and Growing Up
for Kids Ages 9–13

Code #8008 • $12.95

#1 New York Times
BESTSELLING AUTHORS
Jack Canfield
Mark Victor Hansen
Kimberly Kirberger
Raymond Aaron

Chicken Soup for the **Parent's Soul**

Stories of Loving,
Learning and Parenting

Code #7478 • $12.95

#1 New York Times
BESTSELLER
Jack Canfield
Mark Victor Hansen
Kimberly Kirberger

Chicken Soup for the **TEENAGE Soul III**

More Stories of Life, Love
and Learning

Code #7613 • $12.95

Selected titles are also available in hardcover, audiocassette and CD.
Available wherever books are sold.
To order direct: Phone 800.441.5569 • Online www.hci-online.com
Prices do not include shipping and handling. Your response code is BKS.

Code #9098 • Paperback • $12.95

"Seldom have I had the pleasure of reading passages written with such grace, precision and power. Leigh Sanders is a new voice that helps us see beyond our self-imposed limitations of fear and anxiety to a new realm of wholeness and love."

—**H. Jackson Brown Jr.**, author, *Life's Little Instruction Book* and *Live and Learn and Pass It On*

Often people come to a point in life where they feel the need to examine how they feel about themselves, about God, and about life and death. This beautifully written and photographed book of reflection will transport readers to a place of peace and calm.

With the overwhelming success of television shows like *Touched by an Angel* and *Beyond Chance*, it's clear that millions of people are seeking reassurance that miracles are possible. For anyone seeking this spiritual connection, or those who are interested in other unexplainable phenomenon, *Angel Watch*, by best-selling author Catherine Lanigan, offers a compelling and inspirational read.

Code #8199 • Paperback • $11.95

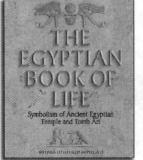

Open the pages of this book and come to know a civilization that embraced life. This beautifully illustrated full-color book will unveil the mysteries and lore of ancient Egypt through elaborate storytelling and the powerful images of more than fifty handcrafted friezes.

Code #8857 • Hardcover• $29.95

Code #9144 • $12.95

Rob Bryant refused to let a paralyzing accident break his spirit or defeat his goal of walking again. Using his inspiring story, Bryant shows how to overcome paralysis—something he defines as any habit, emotion, or fear that keeps you immobilized—and ultimately, face your fears. This compelling personal story is a testament to how faith and courage can triumph in the face of adversity.

Available September 2001

Code #9101 • $12.95

Human Moments is unlike any book available today. Best-selling author and psychiatrist, Edward Hallowell proposes a simple, effective way to find happiness and love by teaching how to recognize human moments when they happen, how to savor them, treasure them, and turn them into an enriching experience. *Human Moments* is an unforgettable book that will awaken hearts and change lives.

Available September 2001

Code #925X • $12.95

In *The 7 Systems of Balance*, renowned psychiatrist Dr. Paul Sorgi, reveals a breakthrough approach to achieving a fully balanced life. In simple, common sense language, Dr. Sorgi helps you to understand what really triggers feelings of imbalance, what's going on in your brain and body and, most importantly, what you can do to correct and prevent the emotional dizziness that can engulf you.

Available September 2001

Available wherever books are sold.
To order direct: Phone 800.441.5569 • Online www.hci-online.com
Prices do not include shipping and handling. Your response code is BKS.

Each of us must travel the ten journeys of life. We must find the paths to maturity, family, prosperity and good health. This book is a treasure trove of wisdom on how to live a full and successful life.

Available August 2001

Code #9233 • $10.95

This beautifully written book details a process that has rarely been exposed before. *The Get* is the story of a woman's journey through love, divorce, spirituality, empowerment and, finally, self-discovery.

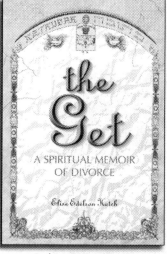

Available September 2001

Code #9292 • $10.95